Unforgettable Presentations That Can Change The World

Presentation techniques that will transform a speech into a memorable event

"Practical, proven techniques that will help you to make your next speech a success"

Dr. Jim Anderson

Published by:
Blue Elephant Consulting
Tampa, Florida

Printed in the United States of America

Library of Congress Control Number: 2018905234

ISBN-13: 978-1717512420
ISBN-10: 1717512429

Warning – Disclaimer

The purpose of this book is to educate and entertain. This book does not promise or guarantee that anyone following the ideas, tips, suggestions, techniques or strategies will be hired. It is the discretion of employers if you will or will not be hired. The author, publisher and distributor(s) shall have neither liability nor responsibility to anyone with respect to any loss or damage caused, or alleged to be caused, directly or indirectly by the information contained in this book.

Recent Books By The Author

Product Management

- Developing World Class Products: Techniques For Product Managers To Better Understand What Their Customers Really Want

- Managing Your Product Manager Career: How Product Managers Can Find And Succeed In The Right Job

Public Speaking

- Creating Speeches That Work: How To Create A Speech That Will Make Your Message Be Remembered Forever!

- How To Organize A Speech In Order To Make Your Point: How to put together a speech that will capture and hold your audience's attention

CIO Skills

- How CIOs Can Bring Business And IT Together: How CIOs Can Use Their Technical Skills To Help Their Company Solve Real-World Business Problems

- New IT Technology Issues Facing CIOs: How CIOs Can Stay On Top Of The Changes In The Technology That

Powers The Company

IT Manager Skills

- How IT Managers Can Use New Technology To Meet Today's IT Challenges: Technologies That IT Managers Can Use In Order to Make Their Teams More Productive

- How To Build High Performance IT Teams: Tips And Techniques That IT Managers Can Use In Order To Develop Productive Teams

Negotiating

- The Art Of Packaging A Negotiation: How To Develop The Skill Of Assembling Potential Trades In Order To Get The Best Possible Outcome

- Getting What You Want In A Negotiation By Learning How To Signal: How To Develop The Skill Of Effective Signaling In A Negotiation In Order To Get The Best Possible Outcome

Miscellaneous

- How To Heal A Broken Leg – Fast!: Understanding how to deal with a broken leg in order to start walking again quickly

- How Software Defined Networking (SDN) Is Going To Change Your World Forever: The Revolution In Network Design And How It Affects

Note: See a complete list of books by Dr. Jim Anderson at the back of this book

Acknowledgements

Any book like this one is the result of years of real-world work experience. In my over 25 years of working for 7 different firms, I have met countless fantastic people and I've been mentored by some truly exceptional ones. Although I've probably forgotten some of the people who made me the person that I am today, here is my attempt to finally give them the recognition that they so truly deserve:

- Thomas P. Anderson
- Art Puett
- Bobbi Marshall
- Bob Boggs

Dr. Jim Anderson

This book is dedicated to my wife Lori. None of this would have been possible without her love and support.

Thanks for the best years of my life (so far)...!

Speaking. Negotiating. Managing. Marketing.

Table Of Contents

HOW TO MAKE YOUR NEXT PRESENTATION COUNT..........................9

ABOUT THE AUTHOR 11

CHAPTER 1: HOW BOYS CAN TALK TO GIRLS (AND VISA VERSA)......16

CHAPTER 2: NEVER GIVE A SPEECH WITHOUT HAVING A POTATO ...20

CHAPTER 3: 10 PROFESSIONAL SPEAKING TIPS THAT YOU NEED TO KNOW 25

CHAPTER 4: WHAT IS YOUR BODY TELLING YOUR AUDIENCE? 30

CHAPTER 5: THE HASSLE OF HECKLERS 34

CHAPTER 6: INSIDE THE MIND OF A HECKLER 38

CHAPTER 7: COUNTERSTRIKE: HOW TO DEAL WITH HECKLERS 42

CHAPTER 8: WHAT AMERICAN IDOL CAN TEACH SPEAKERS (IT'S NOT WHAT YOU THINK) 46

CHAPTER 9: NEVER BE LONELY AGAIN: HOW TO INCLUDE YOUR AUDIENCE IN YOUR SPEECH 51

CHAPTER 10: DO FIRST IMPRESSIONS COUNT WHEN YOU ARE SPEAKING? 55

CHAPTER 11: PUT YOUR HANDS IN THE AIR AND WAVE THEM LIKE YOU DON'T CARE...59

CHAPTER 12: WHEN DISASTER STRIKES: 3 WAYS TO AVOID A CRASH WHILE SPEAKING...63

How To Make Your Next Presentation Count

Every time we give a speech, we all want the same thing to happen. We want to change the world. However, in order to do that we are going to have to find ways to connect with our audience. The challenge that we are facing is that it turns out that this is not an easy thing to do.

For one thing, our audience is not all made up of the same person. In fact, in just about every audience that you'll be presenting to there will be both boys and girls. What this means for you is that you are going to have to craft your speech to appeal to both of them.

In order to give a really good speech, you are going to have to get creative. The good thing is that there are other speakers out there who do this speaking thing for a living. They are more than willing to share their best tips with us in order to help us become better.

As speakers we need to understand that not every time that we give a speech will it be well received by all members of our audience. In fact, some members of our audience may take it upon themselves to start to heckle us even as we speak. It then becomes our obligation to know how to respond when this happens. We're giving a speech for our entire audience, the actions of a one or a few members of that audience cannot be allowed to ruin our speech.

In order to become better speakers we need to be looking for examples of how we can become better. Television shows such as American Idol can provide us with the insights that we are looking for. We need to keep in mind that during every speech that we give, we want to find a way to include our audience.

What our audience thinks about us can be formed from the moment that we take the stage. This is why first impressions can be so important. During our speech, in order to keep our audience engaged in the speech, we need to master the art of using hand gestures. Although we'd like to think that we are in control of how our speech goes, the reality is that disaster can strike at any time. We need to be prepared and ready to deal with it when it comes.

For more information on what it takes to be a great public speaker, check out my blog, The Accidental Communicator, at:

www.TheAccidentalCommunicator.com

Good luck!

- Dr. Jim Anderson

About The Author

I must confess that I never set out to be a public speaker. When I went to school, I studied Computer Science and thought that I'd get a nice job programming and that would be that. Well, at least part of that plan worked out!

My first job was working for Boeing on their F/A-18 fighter jet program. I spent my days programming fighter jet software in assembly language and I loved it. The U.S. government decided to save some money and went looking for other countries to sell this plane to. This put me into an unfamiliar role: I started to meet with foreign military officials and I ended up having to give speeches in order to explain what my product did.

Time moved on and so did I. I found myself working for Siemens, the big German telecommunications company. They were making phone switches and selling them to the seven U.S. phone companies. The problem was that the switches were too complicated. Customers couldn't tell the difference between one complicated phone switch from another complicated phone switch. Once again I found myself standing in front of the room giving speeches in order to explain what these complicated machines did and why ours were better than anyone else's.

I've spent over 25 years working as a product manager for both big companies and startups. This has given me an opportunity to do many, many presentations for customers, at conferences, and everywhere in-between.

I now live in Tampa Florida where I spend my time managing my consulting business, Blue Elephant Consulting, teaching college courses at the University of South Florida, and traveling to work with companies like yours to share the knowledge that I have about how to create and deliver powerful and effective speeches.

I'm always available to answer questions and I can be reached at:

Dr. Jim Anderson
Blue Elephant Consulting
Email: jim@BlueElephantConsulting.com
Facebook: http://goo.gl/1TVoK
Web: **www.BlueElephantConsulting.com**

"Unforgettable communication skills that will set your ideas free..."

Create Speeches That Motivate Your Audiences And Get Your Message Heard!

Dr. Jim Anderson is available to provide training and coaching on the topics that are the most important to people who have to speak in public: how can I create a speech that people want to hear and how can I deliver in a way that will allow me to connect with my audience and get my point across to them?

Dr. Anderson believes that in order to both learn and remember what he says, speakers need to laugh. Each one of his speeches is full of fun and humor so that what he says "sticks" with everyone.

Dr. Anderson's Public Speaking Training Includes:

1. How to plan your next speech: pick your purpose and understand your audience.
2. What's the best way to get PowerPoint and Keynote to work with you, not against you?
3. What do you need to do when you are presenting in order to truly connect with your audience?

Dr. Jim Anderson presents over 100 speeches per year. To invite Dr. Anderson to speak at your event, contact him at: **Phone: 813-418-6970** or **Email: jim@BlueElephantConsulting.com**

CLEAR BLUE Presentation System(tm)

Deliver

Process flow: Plan → Organize → Create → Demo → Rehearse → Present → Change

Prepare

Plan	Organize	Create	Demo	Rehearse	Present	Change
Purpose	Qualifications	Research	Purpose	7x Practice	Intro	Next Time
Audience	Outline	Edit	Outcomes	Credibility	Q&A	Feedback
Speech Type		Plot / Story	Anticipate		Checklist	
		Review				

1 Take-Away	Strong Opening	Strong Close	Preparation	Timing	Nerves	Collection
	Middle to Close	Text	Script	Movements & Gestures	Make Friends	Discussion
		Color	Limited Scope	Energy	The Role of Slides	
		Images & Positioning			3 Components	

Blue Elephant Consulting

www.BlueElephantConsulting.com / 813.418.6970

Blue Elephant Consulting has created the **Clear Blue™ Presentation System** for creating and delivering powerful and memorable presentations. The contents of this book are based on lessons learned during the development of the Clear Blue system. Contact Blue Elephant Consulting to learn more about the Clear Blue presentation system.

Chapter 1

_____

How Boys Can Talk To Girls
(And Visa Versa)

Chapter 1: How Boys Can Talk To Girls (And Visa Versa)

Man, as though giving a speech wasn't hard enough already, then you go ahead and throw **that gender thing** in there and all of a sudden it gets that much tougher! It can be a challenge when you are asked to talk to an audience made up of members of the opposite gender. How can you not screw-up this speech?

Boys Talking To Girls

Male presenters need to adapt their speeches when they are presenting to a primarily female audience. Neil Chethik has a great deal of experience presenting to female audiences and he points out that even in the enlightened age in which we are living, there are still **differences between the sexes** and a skillful presenter has to know about these differences and find ways to steer around them.

- **R-e-s-p-e-c-t:** A male presenter needs to treat his female audience with respect if he wants to have any chance of the speech going well. Women are generally willing to learn from a male presenter; however, they have to feel as though they are being respected.

- **Down To Earth:** A man who starts off his presentation by telling his audience how wonderful he is will instantly lose the connection with his female audience. There's no problem with you being an expert in your area, you just don't want to come off as being a know-it-all. You can connect with your audience by telling a story that points out a personal failing or error and a female audience will connect with you.

- **Evidence Counts:** One of the biggest errors that male presenters make when they are speaking to an all-

16

female audience is that they give an emotional presentation and leave out all of the facts. Yes, women do like stories; however, they won't believe what you are saying unless you can back it up with hard evidence – facts & stats.

- **Humor:** talk about a minefield! Many a good speech to a female audience has gone wrong when the male speaker tried to interject some humor. Your best bet is to let the humor naturally flow from the stories that you are telling. Trying to work in one-liners can only lead to disaster.

Girls Talking To Boys

Yes, men have it rough when they try to address an all-female audience. However, women have it **at least as rough** and perhaps even rougher when they are called on to present to an all-male audience. Once again, there are several ways to make sure that this type of speech goes well:

- **Stand Up:** One of the simplest issues for a woman to solve when she's addressing a male audience is to make sure that they can see her. All too often, a lectern can overwhelm a speaker and hid her from her audience. Stand on something if needed and adjust the mic so that it works correctly for your height.

- **No Expression Is Good:** Often women speakers will become flustered because no matter what they say, the expressions on their male audience won't change. It turns out that this is very normal – men don't tend to display their emotions.

- **Be A Straight Shooter:** Whereas women tend to enjoy hearing lots of stories, men tend to be more "to the point". Clearly communicating your main points and making sure that any stories that you do tell quickly come to the point will help to hold their attention.

- **Be A Professional**: Men do a good job of dealing with other men. They will struggle with any presenter who comes off as being too "girlish". This impression can be caused by clothing, gestures, or even a vocal tone that takes away from what you have to say. Ask a male friend that you trust for help in order to make sure that this is not a problem.

Final Thoughts

Giving any presentation can be a challenge. When it is complicated by the additional challenge of having one gender present to the other gender, it can get even **trickier**.

The key to making this type of speech a success is for the presenter to **acknowledge the situation** and adjust the presentation to match it. Men have to make sure that they show respect to their female audience and women need to not get flustered by their male audience's lack of outward emotions.

Speakers who take the time to adjust what they are going to say and how they are going to say it when addressing the opposite gender will be able to intimately connect with your audience and make a **lasting impact** in their lives.

Chapter 2

Never Give A Speech Without Having A Potato

Chapter 2: Never Give A Speech Without Having A Potato

Bored audiences will get up and **walk out of your speeches**. How would you keep the attention of 400+ engineers who were attending an industry dinner event that they didn't really want to be at on a weekday evening? I recently had the opportunity to be the master of ceremonies at such an event – great gig, tough crowd.

The banquet's master of ceremonies (MC) last year had tried very hard, but had ended up not being able to hold the crowd's attention and they had started to leave before the event was even half over. This year's planning committee presented me with a challenge: find a way to keep the audience in their seats until the end of the event. It turns out that a **single large baking potato** was a key part of my solution to this problem...

Not A Speech, But Rather A 3-Act Play

Two weeks before the banquet was to be held, I had a meeting with the planning committee. The banquet is an annual event for all of the engineers involved in transportation in the Tampa, Florida area. I had been asked to be a co-MC for the event in order to help make it a success. The trouble was that **I know next to nothing about the transportation industry**.

The other MC knew a lot about the industry having worked in it for **over 25 years**. This was a perfect pairing – his smarts and my creativity held the key to our potential success.

The planning committee wanted to focus on the future of transportation in Florida. Since this was **not a typical speech**, there wasn't a speech to prepare. Instead I was looking at creating a play with three acts: an opening, then a second act after the banquet's first speaker, but before its second speaker.

Finally, there would be a third act that would close out the evening.

The Initial Plan: Potatoes Everywhere

Never one to be at a loss for ideas, my initial plan to the team was to propose **other forms of transportation** that people may not have thought of: catapults, rocket launchers, etc.

I took my plan one step further and proposed that we get someone to come up from the audience, put an apron on them, and then have them try to carry as many potatoes as possible across the stage. They would end up dropping some and we could say that a better transportation system was called for.

I had **other ideas that involved the same potatoes**: have planning committee members stand on one side of the stage and try to throw them into a bucket held by another committee member. Lots of potatoes were going to get hurt doing all of this.

In the end, the planning committee **flatly rejected my potato idea**. The possibility of someone getting hurt was just too great and it was sending a negative message about the transportation solutions that are currently being planned for Tampa. Sadly, I think that they made the right decision.

The Next Plan: Jet Packs

The clock was ticking and we were starting to run out of time. We went back to the drawing board and my co-MC did a web search and found all sorts of images of future transportation systems from the 1940's and 1950's covers of Popular Mechanics and Popular Electronics magazines. **A new idea started to emerge**.

Instead of saying anything negative about Tampa's current transportation plans, how about if we came up with **our own vision of the future of transportation**? Make it so outlandish so that everyone knows that it's not a real plan, but incorporate all of that futuristic stuff that everyone has always believed is coming.

I thought that this was a great idea – with one addition. I wanted to have it all lead up to one thing: **a proposal for a jetpack based transportation future**. Hey, everyone loves jetpacks and engineers especially love 'em. The planning committee agreed and one of the members even agreed to build a mock jetpack for us to use.

What This All Means For You

So how did it all turn out you ask? The evening was a **smashing success**. The audience was riveted to their seats – they had to know how this 3-act play was going to come out. Not a soul left before we told them that the show was over.

My co-MC did a great job of reaching out and **drawing the audience in** using his deep knowledge of the transportation industry. The three-act play did its job by hooking the audience's attention in the first act, extending the story in the second act and building up to a big finish in the third act.

The crowning point of the evening was when my co-MC **brought out the Jetpack model** and put it on and announced that the event was over and he was leaving to go home. That was what the audience had been waiting for!

Oh, and the potato? I had brought one to the event as a backup **just in case things didn't go as planned**. We ended up setting it on the podium and not talking about it, not moving it, not doing anything with it. It drove the audience mad with curiosity: why was the potato there? What were they going to do with it? Talk about holding an audience's attention!

Chapter 3

---

10 Professional Speaking Tips That You Need To Know

Chapter 3: 10 Professional Speaking Tips That You Need To Know

Happy New Year! As we start yet another a new year, you may be asking yourself what is the best way for me to become a better public speaker this year? Taking a crash course in which you immerse yourself in all of the subtle tricks of effective speaking is one way. Giving a million speeches and then studying how both yourself and your audience reacted is another.

The problem with both of these approaches is that they take time. Too much time. A much better way to quickly improve is to find a **professional speaker** who is doing it right and ask them how they do it...

Meet A Pro

Shawn Doyle has been a professional speaker for over 19 years. During that time he's made mistakes. **Lots of mistakes**. The good news for you is that he took the time to remember what he did wrong and made sure that he never repeated a mistake.

He's come up with his list of the "**top 10**" things that you just can't learn in a class. Instead, these are the speaking lessons that all professional speakers end up learning on the road. Since you are reading this, just maybe you'll learn them here and you won't have to learn them the hard way!

10 Tips For Giving A Professional Speech

1. Prepare, Prepare, Prepare: I'm going to bet that I've fooled you on this one: I'm not talking about practicing saying your speech. Instead, I'm talking about taking the time to know your audience: how old are they, what do they do for a living, what are they expecting from you.

2. Become A Space-Man: The effectiveness of your speech will be heavily influenced by where you end up giving it. The room, the lighting, the sound system, etc. will all play a role in determining if you are able to connect with your audience. You need to arrive early and check out the room where you'll be speaking. It will be too late to make any changes if you show up just before you go on.

3. It's All In The Opening: Welcome to the age of instant-everything. We can download movies, cook a complete dinner in a microwave in minutes, and purchase almost anything over the Internet. If the opening for your speech is long, slow, and boring then you'll lose your audience right off the bat. You need to grab them at the start and never let go.

4. Talk With Your Hands: When you are giving a speech, your hands are an incredibly powerful communication tool that you can use to boost the impact of your speech. If you are holding on to something (a pen, a piece of paper) while you talk, then your ability to use this tool is greatly diminished. Keep 'em free!

5. Stop Hiding Behind PowerPoint: Ouch! This one probably hits all of us hard. We've worked hard to make a great set of slides and we love to use them. Stop! You are the presentation, not your slides. Don't use PowerPoint if you can get away with it or use it sparingly if you have to. Don't hide behind your slides.

6. Go For A Walk: All too often speakers will plant themselves behind a lectern and stay there during your entire speech. If you do this, then you will have missed an opportunity to engage your audience by moving around. Use your entire body and where you are standing to emphasize the point that you are currently making.

7. Use Your Own Stories: Forget those "Chicken Soup For The ..." books, when you use someone else's story it comes out much weaker than when you tell your own story. Doyle suggests that you use the following formula for creating and telling a story: story + moral + how it relates to the topic = great story.

8. Never, Ever, Apologize: Too often speakers spend much of their speech apologizing for a wide variety of things: the room being too cold, their slides not being in the right order, etc. Stop it! When you apologize, your audience starts to see you in a different light — a negative light. Just skip the apology and move on.

9. You Must Believe To Achieve: In order for your speech to have an impact on your audience, they are going to have to believe that you believe what you are saying. If you are just mouthing words that you don't fully buy into, then you will come across as insincere and your message will have no lasting impact.

10. Think About Your Audience: All too often we write the speeches that we'd like to hear. The problem with this is that we are not necessarily the same as our audience. Your speech must be about your audience and what they want, not about you and what you want.

What All This Means For You

As long as you are going to go to the effort of creating and delivering a speech, you may as well **do a good job of it**. The challenge that we all face is finding ways to become better at giving our speeches so that we can have a greater impact on our audience.

There are a lot of different ways to go about improving our skills; however, one of the simplest and best ways is to **get**

guidance from professionals who have already gone out there and learned the lessons that you want to know.

I've listed 10 suggestions from a pro that should go a long way in helping you to avoid making some of the **more common mistakes that speakers make**. Read, learn, and get out there and speak like a pro!

Chapter 4

What Is Your Body Telling Your Audience?

Chapter 4: What Is Your Body Telling Your Audience?

Did you know that when you are delivering a speech, there is always another conversation going on? No, I'm not talking about your rude audience (although they may be talking also), instead **I'm talking about your body** – it's having its own conversation with your audience. Maybe you should know what it's saying...?

The fact that we are always communicating with our audience through body language should come as no surprise to anyone. However, what might catch your attention is that most of what you think that you know about how to read body language **is probably wrong**. It's just urban myths that have been told over and over again.

A quick example might help me to make my point: what's the best way to make a first impression with someone? If you're like me, you'll assume that greeting them with a lot of energy will show spunk and drive – all good things. **It turns out that we'd be wrong**. Dave Zielinski has been looking into this and he reports that most people believe that people who are low energy and restrained have the most self-confidence.

There is nothing that we can do about preventing our body language from sending messages to our audience. However, the one thing that we can do is **learn to read other people's body language more effectively**.

Common Myths

Have you ever had to give a speech early in the morning? The 900 lb gorilla in the room is the fact that **everyone is still sleepy** – several of them have probably not even woken up yet. What's the best way to get some energy into the room?

30

If you are like most speakers, you'll rely on what we've all been told is the best way to wake up an audience: hit them with a high-energy presentation delivered at a loud volume. It turns out that this is exactly the **wrong thing** to do. Instead, what you need to do is to start out at their energy level (low) and then gradually raise the energy up and allow them to come along with you.

How about when we see people in our audience who have their arms crossed over their chest? They must be **resisting our message**, right? Probably wrong – check the temperature in the room – they may just be cold!

In the end, once you get comfortable understanding what your audience's body language is really telling you, you've got to adjust your body language so that **they can connect with you**. What really matters in your speech is not a lot of body language rules, but rather your voice quality & variation, conviction, strong content, and good eye contact.

What All Of This Means For You

Body language is something that every speaker needs to be aware of. However, we also have to understand that we are probably interpreting it incorrectly because it's **so hard to read**. Don't spent too much time trying to follow a set of body language "rules" because it will take away from your speech.

Instead, do what comes naturally to you. This will allow you to more fully focus on giving the best speech possible and you won't get tripped up trying to remember **a long list of do's and don'ts**.

In the end, if you can allow your body and mind to deliver the same speech then your audience will get a consistent message and you'll be successful in **connecting with your audience**.

Chapter 5

The Hassle Of Hecklers

Chapter 5: The Hassle Of Hecklers

Just imagine your next presentation. You've studied your audience, researched your topic, created a speech, and practiced, practiced, practiced. You take the stage and start to smoothly deliver your speech. Just a few minutes into your speech, you become aware of someone, gasp, talking. We're not talking about quiet whispering here, we're talking about someone in the audience standing up and shouting things at you. Congratulations, **you've got a** heckler**...**

Why Do People Heckle Us?

It's in the world of stand-up comedy that I suspect we are most accustomed to seeing hecklers in real life. That environment has an explosive mix of edgy humor, alcohol, and an audience who desperately wants to show off for friends and participate in the fun. **Hecklers are an everyday part of that environment.** But what about when you are giving a speech?

Just exactly what is a heckler? I'm going to define a heckler as being anyone who chooses to **interrupt your speech** with their own comments. More often than not, a heckler is motivated by deep-set emotions: hostility, resentment, or even simple anger. Whatever you are talking about has set them off and they're not going to be quiet about it. Oh, and there's one more thing – they just might be disagreeing with what you are saying.

As bad as all of this is, there is one more reason that you may have attracted a heckler – **they may not like you.** For whatever reason, there are people out there who will simply set their minds to not liking us for some unknown reason and during our presentation they'll just stand up and let us know about it. Talk about poor timing!

The Best Defense Against A Heckler Is...

The now classic case of how **NOT** to handle a heckler was demonstrated by Michael Richards ("Kramer" on the TV show Seinfeld) when he was performing at comedy club. A table of Afro-American and Hispanic audience members started to heckle him and he responded by trying to "out heckle" them by using racial slurs. Needless to say this didn't work and the fallout from this event is still being felt by him even today.

When it comes to dealing with a heckler, a speaker's options are somewhat limited. What is going on here is **a power play** – you own the stage, but the heckler is trying to take over your audience. The big unanswered question is which way will the audience go – will they side with the heckler or will they side with you, the speaker.

In order to win your audience over to your side, there are **three different things** that you can do:

- **Ignore:** It takes a great deal of courage to be a heckler. If the speaker doesn't acknowledge the heckler and he starts to get disapproving looks and "shsss" sounds from people sitting around him, then his courage will start to fade quickly. By simply ignoring a heckler, you can often get them to sit down and go away quietly.

- **Respond:** another way of saying this is to meet force with force. If your heckler is simply unable to restrain themselves from asking a question, then answer it and go on. If your heckler is being insulting, insult them right back and tell them to sit down and shut-up.

- **Joke:** Humor is a very powerful tool for speakers to use. If you take a moment, and then use humor to either deal with the issue that the heckler has raised or to deal with the heckler himself / herself, then you can defuse the situation and move on.

What All Of This Means For You

At some point in your speaking career, you will be confronted with a heckler. It's how you **choose to deal with this interruption** that will define how good of a speaker you are.

It's all too easy to **over react** when someone has been rude enough to interrupt your speech. You've got a number of options from ignoring them to using humor to deflect the interruption. How you handle it will depend on the circumstances that you find yourself in.

The ultimate goal is to keep the audience on your side and **not have them bond with the heckler**. If you treat every interruption with dignity and style, you'll have won the audience over and you'll be seen as the great speaker that you can be.

Chapter 6

Inside The Mind Of A Heckler

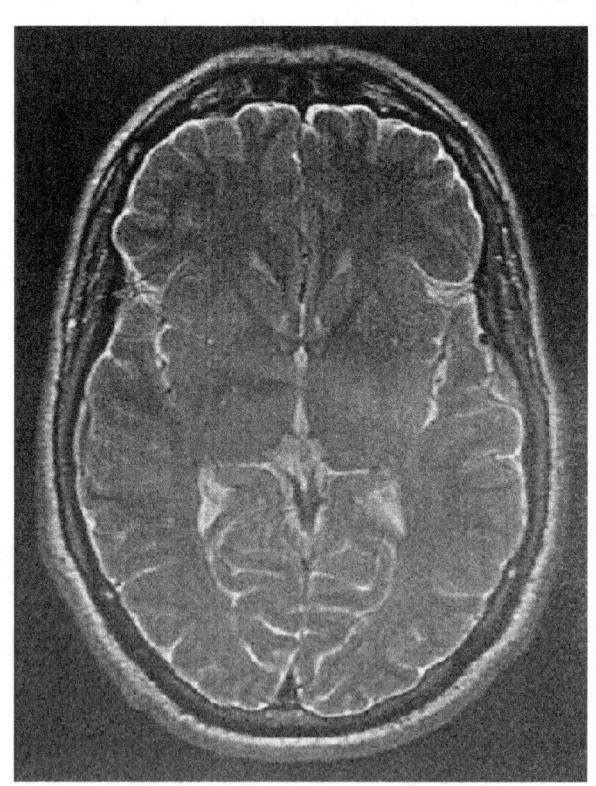

Chapter 6: Inside The Mind Of A Heckler

If you could **wish for just one thing** before you give your next speech in public, what would it be? Sure we'd all like to be able to talk like Tony Robbins, move a crowd like Zig Ziglar, or even have a powerful story to tell like Rudy Giuliani. However, I'm willing to bet good money that after considerable thought, we'd all settle for spending our wish on making sure that there were no hecklers in the audience.

The reason that speakers fear hecklers so much isn't that they are so rude. Rather **it's an issue of control** – we have it and they want it. The person up on the stage who is speaking (that's you) "owns" the crowd. When a heckler starts to harass you, they are trying to wrestle control of the crowd away from you.

In order to start to find out how to deal with hecklers, the very first step is to take a step back and understand just who they are. It turns out that they (normally) are not wild-eyed radicals. Instead, **they are very much people just like you and me**. They are speaking up because they are feeling enormous pressure for some reason. This leads to a feeling of being powerless, intimidated, uncomfortable, or simply being overlooked. This is what is what turns them into a heckler.

It's very easy for a speaker to **lose control** when a heckler starts to verbally assault them. However, you need to realize that when a heckler starts to speak, very quickly the audience will recognize them for what they are – a disruption.

Why Do They Do It?

Judi Bailey has looked into the psychology behind why people become hecklers. She reports that mental health experts agree that a heckler's disorderly conduct is a symptom of **an unmet need**.

Just what kind of unmet need they are dealing with will determine what action you will need to take. Judi has created an acronym, **H-O-S-T-I-L-E** that can help speakers to quickly classify the type of heckler that they are dealing with:

Heckler: these are the ones who are simply being rude to you. The reason that they are doing this is because they have a feeling of low personal worth and they are trying to build themselves up by getting into a shouting match with you.

Over-zealous: a strong need for approval causes this type of heckler to always want to lead a conversation. They'll show up most often if you ask the audience a question – they will be the one who wants to answer it before anyone else.

Squawker: the ultimate source of negativity, this type of heckler will poo-poo any idea or proposal. The reason that they are doing this is because it's easy to do (doesn't take a lot of thinking to say "no" to a new idea) and because they desperately need acknowledgement.

Turned-Off: the heckler who isn't confronting you directly, but who is doing something else – like having a phone call in the middle of your speech. This may be partly your fault because they very clearly have an unmet need for connection.

Intimidator: it's all about power for this type of heckler. They are more than willing to sit through a speech as long as they are the ones doing the speaking. They are easy to spot because the vocabulary that they will use will be aggressive.

Lost: another way to refer to this heckler is "clueless". For whatever reason they're just not "getting" what you're talking about and so they can keep asking the same pointless questions. Clearly this type of heckler has a need for either a direction to go in or information that they can use.

Expert: we've all seen this one before – he / she thinks that they know more than the speaker (and they may) and they're going to let everyone else know it. What we're looking at here is a clear need for personal recognition.

What All Of This Means For You

I'm sorry to report that to the best of my knowledge, **there are no magic wishes available to speakers**. This means that you'll never be able to start a speech with the guarantee that you won't interrupted by a heckler.

The key point that you always need to keep in mind is that no matter how inappropriate their behavior is, they are generally just people like you and me. However, because of their current situation **they feel compelled to speak out**.

Realizing that there are different types of hecklers is the first step in **learning to deal with them**. Once you are able to classify the type of heckler that you are dealing with, you'll be well on your way to making sure that control of your speech stays firmly in your hands.

Chapter 7

Counterstrike: How To Deal With Hecklers

Chapter 7: Counterstrike: How To Deal With Hecklers

Nothing makes me more angry than when someone is rude enough to interrupt me when I'm giving a speech. I mean come on, I've worked hard to prepare to give this speech and here I am dealing with all of the nerves, logistics, etc. that a speaker needs to stay on top of and all of a sudden I have to put up with this? There has got to be a way to get this person to **shut up and sit down**, right?

Preparing For A Fight

The best way to deal with a heckler is to do your best to **prevent them from becoming a heckler in the first place**. A heckler can show up in any audience and so as part of your preparation to give a speech, you need to spend some time taking steps to defuse the things that might set a heckler off. Judi Bailey has done some research into just exactly what you can do and she's got the following suggestions:

Research Your Audience: The easiest way to invite a hacker to attack you is to not take the time to understand who you'll be presenting to. A key part of this understanding is to make sure that you know who in the audience will be supporting what you have to say, and who you need to watch out for.

Double Check Your Data: The Achilles heel that trips up most speakers when it comes to dealing with hecklers lies in the information that you are presenting. If you aren't careful and you present information that is either incorrect or out of date, then you will have opened a door for hecklers to attack.

Watch Your Time: When are you going to be delivering your speech? If it's in the morning, then your audience is going to be fresh and ready to listen to more detailed information. However, the later in the day that you go, the less willing your audience is going to be to absorb the data that you've based your speech on.

Mind Your Purpose: One of the key ways to negate the impact of a heckler is for you to stay focused on what really matters to your audience. By making sure that what you are talking about is what they want to hear you'll be able to keep everyone's attention and reduce the chance that a heckler will rise to the surface.

Dealing With A Fight When It Happens

Even with all of the best preparation in the world, you will still get **the occasional heckler**. That means that you need to have a plan for dealing with them when they show up. Judi has the following suggestions for defusing these volatile situations:

Establish Guidelines: At the start of your speech you have a unique opportunity to layout some guidelines for everyone to follow. These guidelines can include telling everyone what topics will and won't be covered, what people should do if they object to what you are saying, and explaining if there will be an opportunity to ask questions during your presentation.

Be Like A Ninja: If you do have a heckler stand up and take issue with something that you've said, then you have an opportunity to use your built-in ninja skills to deal with the situation. The simplest way to deal with a heckler is to side-step their comments. This means that you need to deal with the heckler, then step to the side to show the audience that you are moving on and keep on speaking.

Take Them On: This is sort of the nuclear option for speakers – dealing directly with a heckler. Clearly there are all sorts of risks associated with this approach; however, it can be the most direct and decisive way to move beyond the distraction that a heckler is causing. Keep in mind that your goal is to deliver the most value to the audience, not to embarrass the heckler. Acknowledge their point, tell them to sit down, and move on.

What All Of This Means For You

Every public speaker needs to realize that hecklers **come with the territory**. Preparing to deal with them before a speech starts is the key to boosting your odds of successfully dealing with them.

You need to take steps as you prepare to deliver your speech and as you start to talk to your audience in order to **minimize the chances** of a heckler standing up and causing a disruption.

No matter how you choose to deal with a heckler, **they are your responsibility**. Realizing that you can't make them go away, the next best thing that we can all do is to be ready to deal with them when they do show up...

Chapter 8

What American Idol Can Teach Speakers (It's Not What You Think)

Chapter 8: What American Idol Can Teach Speakers (It's Not What You Think)

I'm pretty sure that by now everyone has at least heard about the TV show "American Idol". It's the most popular show on television right now and everyone seems to be talking and gossiping about it all the time. Outside of being a great source of entertainment, is it possible that this show just might be able to teach us a few things about **how to become a better speaker...?**

Sure They Can Sing, But So What?

I've known about American Idol since it first showed up something like nine years ago. However, I had not understood **its value to a speaker** until I visited Disney World the other week. At Disney's Hollywood theme park, they have an attraction called, what else, "America Idol". You sit in the audience and three amateur singers compete to win the audience's vote.

It was the fact that the performers were such rank amateurs and that I got to see them up close and in person that finally drove home what I had been missing. Look, all three of the competitors were better singers than I am (that's not really saying all that much), but I don't think that it was their voice **that determined who won.**

None of the three young ladies that were performing on the day that I attended the show were all that good. I mean, they had nice voices and all that, but would they make it on to the TV show – probably not. In fact, I'd say that their voices and singing ability were all pretty much equal. **So what set them apart from each other?**

It turns out that their **stage presence** is what really set these three performers apart. The first young lady came out and sang. She did a very nice job, but she just stood there and belted out her tune. From an audience perspective, we all enjoyed it and assumed that the other two performers would do the same.

However, when the second performer came out, not only did she sing but she also **moved around on the stage** as she sang. The difference was quite startling – the audience really responded to her song. Finally the third performer came out and not only sang and moved around on the stage, but you could see in her body language that she was "feeling" the emotion in the song that she was singing.

I probably don't have to tell you who won – the third singer. From a speaker point-of-view the difference between how **the audience responded** to the three different singers was amazing. It really drove home the understanding that any speech that we give is really a performance and that we need to use our whole body in order to really connect with our audience.

Why Simon Is So Popular

If that was all that I had learned at this show, then I would have felt that I had gotten more than my money's worth for my $74 Disney ticket. However, this show had **one more lesson** to teach me.

On the TV show there are three judges that evaluate the contestants. One of these judges is **Simon Cowell**. He has become famous for being mean – if someone's performance is not very good, then Simon won't mince any words and will tell them that they are a terrible singer and that they should go home.

Millions of people watch the show **just to hear what Simon is going to say next**. They hate him for making people feel bad and cry, but they love him for being willing to speak his mind at the same time. At the Disney show they had a stand-in for Simon who spoke with an Australian accent (Simon speaks with a British accent) and he played the part very well – he insulted all three singers.

What caught my attention was just how important a part of the show the Simon figure was. It wouldn't have been American Idol without him. The audience knew what he was going to say, but still there was **an eager anticipation to hear him each time he spoke**.

Watching all of this unfold I was struck with the realization that you don't need to have your audience like you or even like what you are talking about. However, you do need to have **a very clearly defined position.**

If people know what you stand for then **they'll pay attention to you**. They may be listening to get confirmation of their own beliefs or they may be listening in order to confirm that they think that you are wrong. It doesn't matter – they are still listening to you!

What All Of This Means For You

We may never have an opportunity to appear on the TV show "American Idol" and bask in the glory of millions of adoring fans. However, that doesn't mean that the show can't make our lives better by **teaching us a thing or two.**

When the voices are roughly the same, the thing that sets performers apart is how they use their bodies **to support the words that they are saying**. Speakers need to learn to do the same thing. Simon Cowell and his sharp personality is a key part of the show's success. Speakers who have a well-defined position will always be able to keep the attention of their audiences.

As speakers we can learn from all of the nervousness and embarrassment that the singers on this show have to go through (including having to be evaluated by Simon!). Applying what works for singers can help all of us to become better speakers.

Chapter 9

Never Be Lonely Again: How To Include Your Audience In Your Speech

Chapter 9: Never Be Lonely Again: How To Include Your Audience In Your Speech

Let's face it – anyone can give a speech. However, not anyone can give a good speech. It sure seems as though if you're going to go to all of the effort of preparing and delivering a speech, you sure would like to do a good job of it. That means that you're going to have to find a way to **really connect with your audience**. Guess what – it turns out that this is actually pretty easy to do. The trick is that you have to start to use more "people words" when you speak…

It's All About How You Say Things

Once you understand what I'm talking about this is going to be a simple concept – it's just that it may be a bit difficult for me to explain. Let's start our discussion by thinking back to the last time that you sat down to create a speech. I'm sure that what was front and center in your mind as you wrote your speech was **the point that you were trying to make by giving the speech**. There's no problem with this.

Where we run into problems is when you sit back and take a look at the speech that you've written: I'm willing to bet you that **it's pretty cold and impersonal**. Don't get me wrong, you've probably did a great job of getting your main point across; however, it's not going to be an effective speech because you're not going to be able to connect with your audience.

The way to fix this problem of great speech / lousy connection is to go back and plug in more **"people words"**. These types of words are very clear references to human beings just like you, me, and your audience. The more of these types of words that you can include in your speech, the warmer your speech will appear and the easier it will be to connect with your listeners. Oprah does this all the time.

Kevin Johnston and Tennille-Lynn Millo are writers who use this technique in their work. The most effect technique that they've found to use is to start to ask the question **"who"** when you are reviewing your speech. What you will be trying to do is to replace the impersonal "the sales department" with "Mike and the rest of the team in the Sales department". See how much warmer that is?

The Problem With Statistics

I can already see some of you rolling your eyes – look Dr. Jim, my speech is filled with **facts and stats** – there's nothing warm and personal about it. Well, you've got a point there but never say never. Even this type of speech can be warmed up with some more people words.

Take an ugly stat: about two thirds of U.S. adults are either overweight or obese. Ouch, but who cares – that's cold and impersonal. **How could you warm this one up?** Simple, say something like "If you and your two best friends were in the room with us today, statistics say that that at least two of you would be either overweight or obese". Much better!

Does Anyone Have A Body?

One of the reasons that so many speeches fail to connect with their audience is because what's being discussed **is not human** – and so your audience tunes the discussion out. If you take the time to apply human words to non-human things you'll be able to get your audience's attention back.

The classic phrase **"take a bite out of crime"** is known by everyone. You can apply the same technique by saying "we've got to kick the competition" or "we want to stop crawling towards our goals and get up and start to run."

It's Name Time

The final way to warm your speech up and make a better connection with your audience may be the simplest of them all: **start name dropping**. When you are looking over your speech, search for places where you reference a position or a role and instead of saying "the company's treasurer", replace it with "Tom, the company's treasurer".

If you want to take this up a notch even more, if you can insert names of people who are in your audience **you'll score even more points with them**. This is one of the reasons that the great speakers show up early for a speech and chat with the audience – they are collecting names to use later on in their speech.

What All Of This Means For You

It's all too easy to write a cold and impersonal speech. It might do a good job of discussing our main topic; however, it's going to be a waste of your time to deliver it **if you can't connect with your audience**.

Taking the time to review the speech that you've written and working in "people words" will provide you with the opportunity to **warm your speech up**. Every speech can benefit from this kind of attention including speeches that have lots of statistics.

The more names that you can use in your speech, the more of a connection you'll be able to establish with your audience. If you can work the names of actual audience members into your speech, then you will be well on your way to **becoming a great speaker...**

Chapter 10

Do First Impressions Count When You Are Speaking?

Chapter 10: Do First Impressions Count When You Are Speaking?

I'm not sure if this falls into the "good news" or "bad news" category, but it turns out that your audience **may have already made up their mind about listening to what you have to say** even before you open your mouth to speak. Do I have your attention now?

What The Researchers Have Discovered About First Impressions

We've always been taught that **the opening of a speech** is the most critical part of any speech because it is at that time that you have everyone's attention and they are trying to make up their minds as to whether or not to listen to you. However, researchers are now telling us that that the decision is being made even earlier.

In fact, the audience started making up their minds about you as you got up and **started moving towards the podium**. What happens is that everyone makes a first impression about you upon seeing that you are the speaker (yeah, I know it's not right, but it's what we all do so get over it) and then that first impression is used to interpret everything that you do after that.

This conclusion is not without its detractors. There are some that say that the first impression **is not as strong as many believe**. Others believe that we get a chance to form a second first impression after the first meeting. This may be true, but as speakers we may never get that second chance so we should be careful to make the best first impression possible.

How Can A Speaker's Words Make A Good First Impression?

A million years can pass from when the person who is running the meeting starts to introduce you to when you actually take the stage. During that time **a lot can happen** and you need to make sure that it's all positive. The title of your speech is the first place to start: does it grab the audience's imagination and excite them to hear what you are going to say?

How you take the stage is the next step. If you shuffle onto the stage with your head hanging low looking like you'd really rather be anywhere else in the world than there, your audience will start to wish that they were there also. However, if instead, you project confidence as you stride up and take the stage then your audience will sit up and take notice.

Once you've taken the stage, we're now back to that issue of **the first words that will be tumbling out of your mouth**. Here's an interesting thought: how much time do you spend on the first sentence in your speeches? I'm going to guess that the answer is not enough. This is the million dollar waterfront real estate in your speech – it's worth the investment of time to get it right. You want your words to start a fire in your audience's mind – your opening needs to promise great things to come in the rest of your speech.

If Looks Matter, What Can A Speaker Do?

So clearly people will be making **snap judgements** about you simply based on how you look. Pick your clothes carefully. You want to look sharp and polished. The rule of thumb when giving a speech is that you always want to be the best-dressed person in the room.

Make sure that when you start to speak **you speak in a loud clear voice**. This will tell everyone that you are very confidant and that they should listen to what you have to say. Make sure that your body language is in agreement with the words that are coming out of your mouth. Finally, never forget to smile. When you smile your audience can't help but smile back at you and that will go a long way in winning them over to your side.

What All Of This Means For You

As speakers we like to imagine that our speeches **start when we open our mouth the first time to start speaking**. Research has shown that this is not the case: our audiences are forming first impressions of us long before we reach the stage.

What this means is that we need to make sure that we dress the part and project an air of self-confidence **even before we reach the stage**. Once there, the first words of our speech need to be crafted in order to capture our audience's attention and hold it.

The bad news is that our audiences are prejudging us before we have a chance to show them how good of a speaker we are. The good news is that **now we know that they are doing this** and with a little effort, we can use this knowledge to make sure that we get them to make a positive first impression and then we've got them right where we want them to be.

Chapter 11

Put Your Hands In The Air And Wave Them Like You Don't Care...

Chapter 11: Put Your Hands In The Air And Wave Them Like You Don't Care…

If you've ever gotten any training on how to give a speech, the instructor probably told you that if used correctly, **hand gestures can be a powerful tool**. However, as with all such things in life, do you think that it's possible to use this tool just a bit too much? Where should a speaker draw the line?

The History Of The Hand Gesture

So just where did the idea of using hand gestures to give some more "oomph" to a speech come from? Well, there are a lot of different ideas but the one that seems to hold the most weight is the one that reminds us that **PA systems are a relatively new invention**.

What this means is that back in the day a speaker might not be able to be heard by some (or most) of their audience. At least not everything that they'd say. Clearly this was a problem. In order to at least partially solve this problem, speakers **started to use outsized hand gestures** in order to clearly convey the emotion of the words that that they were speaking at the time.

This means that if you were **getting angry** about something, while you said the words you'd go ahead and start to punch the air in front of you with your fist. This meant that even the people sitting back in the "cheap seats" would get the point that you were ticked off about something.

In all honesty **this made a lot of sense**. Public speaking got its start in the theatrical productions that were popular back in the day. Speaking for a long time was simply a form of acting.

The Day That The Hand Gesture Died

Well, ok, it didn't really die. However, the arrival of the ability to amplify a speaker's voice by using a PA system **changed the nature of public speaking forever**. All of a sudden, those wild hand gestures were no longer needed – everyone could hear you and it was your words that counted, not your hand gestures.

This has all led to where we find ourselves today. Instead of attempting to appear as though we are putting on a one man (or one woman) stage production, what we are all trying to do is find ways to come across as **being as authentic as possible**. This means that we've done away with the windmilling of the arms and instead started to focus more on the words that we say.

This isn't to say that hand gesture are no longer an important part of the toolkit that a speaker has to work with. The trick is to know **when and how** to use them.

A hand gesture should never come across as being **a forced action**. Instead it should bubble up and be interpreted by your audience as a natural extension of what you are saying. It should fit the moment and help to make your point.

What All Of This Means For You

When you watch the video of old-time political leaders, we often have to laugh to ourselves when we see the wild hand gestures that they used. However, if we realize that the reason for those gestures was because more people could see them than hear them, **it all starts to make sense**.

The days of the big hand gestures have gone away; however, that doesn't mean that hand gestures are not still a powerful tool for a public speaker. You just need to be careful how you go about using them. In the end, your hand gestures **should be as authentic as your speech is**.

Chapter 12

When Disaster Strikes: 3 Ways To Avoid A Crash While Speaking

Chapter 12: When Disaster Strikes: 3 Ways To Avoid A Crash While Speaking

Welcome to the real world – things happen. Specially, things happen while you are delivering a speech. Bad things, things that can really screw up your speech. Fire alarms go off, the power fails, a projector bulb quits, your laptop decides to eat itself, etc. What's a speaker to do?

You Need To Have A Plan

If you want to have any chance of **not self-destructing** when something goes wrong while you are giving a speech, then you're going to have to have a plan. Oh, and it's going to have to be a really good plan.

Can you say **homework**? In order to prepare for things to happen while you are giving a speech, you're going to need to spend some time BEFORE the speech running through all of the things that just might happen. Once you've identified these things, you'll start to feel much more relaxed about your actual speech – you should be ready for whatever happens.

A while ago I took advantage of an opportunity that was presented to me to become a Certified Business Continuity Professional. This means that I'm now considered to be **an expert in how to plan for the worst**.

The most important thing that I got out of all of my training was actually the simplest: you need to **identify everything** that could possibly happen to you, but then you only have to plan for the most probable items on that list. Possible fire drill – plan for it. Meteor striking the earth during your speech – put it on the list but don't worry about planning for it (too low of a probability).

It's All About The Escape Hatch

Although you might want to have a hole that you could just go and jump in if something happens to disrupt your presentation, you don't actually have that option. In show business they have a saying that says **"The show must go on"** and the same can be said for your presentation. What you do need to have is an escape hatch that leads from the presentation that you were giving to the one that you will be giving after the event happens.

This means that before your speech, you need to have taken the time and **thought through all of the possible things that could go wrong**. Just thinking about them is not enough, you also need to decide what you would do if they happened. I'd take the time to write down both the possible event as well as the action that you'd take if it happened. Just the action of writing can help to firm things up in your mind.

A case in point: if your projector bulb failed, how would you handle that? One possibility would be to distribute a handout that you had created just for this situation. Another way to handle it would be to bring out the flip chart and to start drawing on it. Doesn't matter what you do, **just have a plan in case something happens**.

You Are The Rock, Act That Way

Any speech is actually **a performance**. When something goes wrong, your performance doesn't end. How you react to an unplanned event will go a long way in determining how your audience reacts to the event.

What all this means is simply that you need to **not react** when something goes wrong. Don't show any surprise, deal with it, and keep on moving forward with your speech.

The hardest part of all of this is remembering that it's not just the words that you are saying that may betray surprise, but also **your body language**. This is once again where having thought though through all of the possibilities will help you deal with them as expected occurrences.

Practice, Practice, Practice

In order to bring all of this planning into operation, you need to have **practiced** what you would do if something happened. I'm not suggesting that you pull a fire alarm or sabotage your projector, my suggestion is much simpler.

After you've gotten done with your planning, sit down and **mentally picture yourself delivering your speech**. Now imagine something going wrong. What do you do? "See" yourself reacting calmly and with a great deal of assurance to whatever the event is.

By mentally running through the event and your reaction to it, you'll build up a **"learned response"**. This means that if such an event does happen to you, you'll instinctively know how to react. Both your words and your body language will be telling your audience that you have the situation well under control.

What All Of This Means For You

Life does sometimes give us lemons. Unfortunately sometimes these lemons arrive **right in the middle of one of our presentations**. How we deal with life's unplanned events can determine the success or failure of that speech.

We must always **pre-plan for events that are out of our control** happening during a speech. This planning will help us to have a back-up plan in place and will allow us to convey a sense of control to our audience.

Yes, this will require more work on your part in order to get ready to give a speech. However, taking the time to plan for the worst to happen can help you deliver a **successful speech** under the worst of circumstances.

It's from the forge of failure that the steel of success is formed.

Hard Work Does Not Guarantee Success, But Success Does Not Happen Without Hard Work.

- Dr. Jim Anderson

Create Speeches That Motivate Your Audiences And Get Your Message Heard!

Dr. Jim Anderson is available to provide training and coaching on the topics that are the most important to people who have to speak in public: how can I create a speech that people want to hear and how can I deliver in a way that will allow me to connect with my audience and get my point across to them?

Dr. Anderson believes that in order to both learn and remember what he says, speakers need to laugh. Each one of his speeches is full of fun and humor so that what he says "sticks" with everyone.

Dr. Anderson's Public Speaking Training Includes:

1. How to plan your next speech: pick your purpose and understand your audience.
2. What's the best way to get PowerPoint and Keynote to work with you, not against you?
3. What do you need to do when you are presenting in order to truly connect with your audience?

Dr. Jim Anderson presents over 100 speeches per year. To invite Dr. Anderson to speak at your event, contact him at: **Phone: 813-418-6970** or **Email: jim@BlueElephantConsulting.com**

Photo Credits:

https://www.flickr.com/photos/andypowe11/

Chapter 7 - William Andrus

https://www.flickr.com/photos/wandrus/

Chapter 8 – Beth

https://www.flickr.com/photos/laundry/

Chapter 9 - Gh0stman

https://www.flickr.com/photos/ghostman/

Chapter 10 - Adam Bornstein

https://www.flickr.com/photos/91655072@N00/

Chapter 11 - Worn Fashion Journal

https://www.flickr.com/photos/wornfashionjournal/

Chapter 12 – perthhdproductions

https://www.flickr.com/photos/perthhdproductions/

Other Books By The Author

Product Management

- Developing World Class Products: Techniques For Product Managers To Better Understand What Their Customers Really Want

- How Product Managers Can Sell More Of Their Product: Tips & Techniques For Product Managers To Better Understand How To Sell Their Product

- How Product Managers Can Sell More Of Their Product: Tips & Techniques For Product Managers To Better Understand How To Sell Their Product

- How To Create A Successful Product That Customers Will Want: Techniques For Product Managers To Boost Product Sales And Increase Customer Satisfaction

- What Product Managers Need To Know About World-Class Product Development: How Product Managers Can Create Successful Products

- How Product Managers Can Learn To Understand Their Customers: Techniques For Product

Managers To Better Understand What Their
Customers Really Want

- Product Management Secrets: Techniques For
  Product Managers To Boost Product Sales And
  Increase Customer Satisfaction

- Product Development Lessons For Product
  Managers: How Product Managers Can Create
  Successful Products

- Customer Lessons For Product Managers:
  Techniques For Product Managers To Better
  Understand What Their Customers Really Want

- Product Failure Lessons For Product Managers:
  Examples Of Products That Have Failed For Product
  Managers To Learn From

- Communication Skills For Product Managers: The
  Communication Skills That Product Managers Need
  To Know How To Use In Order To Have A Successful
  Product

- How To Have A Successful Product Manager
  Career: The Things That You Need To Be Doing
  TODAY In Order To Have A Successful Product
  Manager Career

- Product Manager Product Success: How to keep your product on track and make it become a success

Public Speaking

- Creating Speeches That Work: How To Create A Speech That Will Make Your Message Be Remembered Forever!

- How To Organize A Speech In Order To Make Your Point: How to put together a speech that will capture and hold your audience's attention

- Changing How You Speak To Overcome Your Fear Of Speaking: Change techniques that will transform a speech into a memorable event

- Delivering Excellence: How To Give Presentations That Make A Difference: Presentation techniques that will transform a speech into a memorable event

- Tools Speakers Need In Order To Give The Perfect Speech: What tools to use to create your next speech so that your message will be remembered forever!

- How To Create A Speech That Will Be Remembered

- Secrets To Organizing A Speech For Maximum Impact: How to put together a speech that will capture and hold your audience's attention

- How To Become A Better Speaker By Changing How You Speak: Change techniques that will transform a speech into a memorable event

- How To Give A Great Presentation: Presentation techniques that will transform a speech into a memorable event

- How To Rehearse In Order To Give The Perfect Speech: How to effectively rehearse your next speech to that your message be remembered forever!

- Secrets To Creating The Perfect Speech: How to create a speech that will make your message be remembered forever!

- Secrets To Organizing The Perfect Speech: How to organize the best speech of your life!

- Secrets To Planning The Perfect Speech: How to plan to give the best speech of your life

- How To Show What You Mean During A Presentation: How to use visual techniques to transform a speech into a memorable event

- **CIO Skills**

- How CIOs Can Bring Business And IT Together: How CIOs Can Use Their Technical Skills To Help Their Company Solve Real-World Business Problems

- New IT Technology Issues Facing CIOs: How CIOs Can Stay On Top Of The Changes In The Technology That Powers The Company

- Keeping The Barbarians Out: How CIOs Can Secure Their Department and Company: Tips And Techniques For CIOs To Use In Order To Secure Both Their IT Department And Their Company

- What CIOs Need To Know In Order To Successfully Manage An IT Department: Decision Making Skills That Every CIO Needs To Have In Order To Be Able To Make The Right Choices

- Becoming A Powerful And Effective Leader: Tips And Techniques That IT Managers Can Use In Order To Develop Leadership Skills

- CIO Secrets For Growing Innovation: Tips And Techniques For CIOs To Use In Order To Make Innovation Happen In Their IT Department

- Your Success As A CIO Depends On How Well You Communicate: Tips And Techniques For CIOs To

Use In Order To Become Better Communicators

- What CIOs Need To Know About Working With Partners: Techniques For CIOs To Use In Order To Be Able To Successfully Work With Partners

- Critical CIO Management Skills: Decision Making Skills That Every CIO Needs To Have In Order To Be Able To Make The Right Choices

- How CIOs Can Make Innovation Happen: Tips And Techniques For CIOs To Use In Order To Make Innovation Happen In Their IT Department

- CIO Communication Skills Secrets: Tips And Techniques For CIOs To Use In Order To Become Better Communicators

- Managing Your CIO Career: Steps That CIOs Have To Take In Order To Have A Long And Successful Career

- CIO Business Skills: How CIOs can work effectively with the rest of the company!

- **IT Manager Skills**

- How IT Managers Can Use New Technology To Meet Today's IT Challenges: Technologies That IT Managers Can Use In Order to Make Their Teams

More Productive

- How To Build High Performance IT Teams: Tips
  And Techniques That IT Managers Can Use In Order
  To Develop Productive Teams

- Save Yourself, Save Your Job – How To Manage
  Your IT Career: Secrets That IT Managers Can Use
  In Order To Have A Successful Career

- Growing Your CIO Career: How CIOs Can Work
  With The Entire Company In Order To Be Successful

- How IT Managers Can Make Innovation Happen:
  Tips And Techniques For IT Managers To Use In
  Order To Make Innovation Happen In Their Teams

- Staffing Skills IT Managers Must Have: Tips And
  Techniques That IT Managers Can Use In Order To
  Correctly Staff Their Teams

- Secrets Of Effective Leadership For IT Managers:
  Tips And Techniques That IT Managers Can Use In
  Order To Develop Leadership Skills

- IT Manager Career Secrets: Tips And Techniques
  That IT Managers Can Use In Order To Have A
  Successful Career

- IT Manager Budgeting Skills: How IT Managers Can Request, Manage, Use, And Track Their Funding

- Secrets Of Managing Budgets: What IT Managers Need To Know In Order To Understand How Their Company Uses Money

Negotiating

- The Art Of Packaging A Negotiation: How To Develop The Skill Of Assembling Potential Trades In Order To Get The Best Possible Outcome

- Getting What You Want In A Negotiation By Learning How To Signal: How To Develop The Skill Of Effective Signaling In A Negotiation In Order To Get The Best Possible Outcome

- Exploring How To Get The Deal That You Want In A Negotiation: How To Develop The Skill Of Exploring What Is Possible In A Negotiation In Order To Reach The Best Possible Deal

- Use The Power Of Arguing To Win Your Next Negotiation: How To Develop The Skill Of Effective Arguing In A Negotiation In Order To Get The Best Possible Outcome

- Learn How To Signal In Your Next Negotiation: How To Develop The Skill Of Effective Signaling In A

Negotiation In Order To Get The Best Possible
Outcome

- Learn The Skill Of Exploring In A Negotiation: How
  To Develop The Skill Of Exploring What Is Possible
  In A Negotiation In Order To Reach The Best
  Possible Deal

- Learn How To Argue In Your Next Negotiation: How
  To Develop The Skill Of Effective Arguing In A
  Negotiation In Order To Get The Best Possible
  Outcome|

- How To Open Your Next Negotiation: How To Start
  A Negotiation In Order To Get The Best Possible
  Outcome

- Preparing For Your Next Negotiation: What You
  Need To Do BEFORE A Negotiation Starts In Order
  To Get The Best Possible Deal

- Learn How To Package Trades In Your Next
  Negotiation

- All Good Things Come To An End: How To Close A
  Negotiation - How To Develop The Skill Of Closing
  In Order To Get The Best Possible Outcome From A
  Negotiation

- Take No Prisoners In Your Next Negotiation: How To Start A Negotiation In Order To Get The Best Possible Outcome

Miscellaneous

- How To Heal A Broken Leg – Fast!: Understanding how to deal with a broken leg in order to start walking again quickly

- How Software Defined Networking (SDN) Is Going To Change Your World Forever: The Revolution In Network Design And How It Affects You

- The Power Of Virtualization: How It Affects Memory, Servers, and Storage: The Revolution In Creating Virtual Devices And How It Affects You

- The Internet-Enabled Successful School District Superintendent: How To Use The Internet To Boost Parental Involvement In Your Schools

- Power Distribution Unit (PDU) Secrets: What Everyone Who Works In A Data Center Needs To Know!

- Making The Jump: How To Land Your Dream Job When You Get Out Of College!

- How To Use The Internet To Create Successful Students And Involved Parents

"Presentation techniques that will transform a speech into a memorable event"

This book has been written with one goal in mind – to show you how you can present a powerful and effective speech. We're going to show you how to use the tools that every speaker has to deliver a great speech!

Let's Make Your Next Speech A Success!

<u>**What You'll Find Inside:**</u>

- **HOW BOYS CAN TALK TO GIRLS (AND VISA VERSA)**

- **10 PROFESSIONAL SPEAKING TIPS THAT YOU NEED TO KNOW**

- **COUNTERSTRIKE: HOW TO DEAL WITH HECKLERS**

- **WHEN DISASTER STRIKES: 3 WAYS TO AVOID A CRASH WHILE SPEAKING**

Dr. Jim Anderson brings his 25 years of real-world experience to this book. He's delivered speeches at some of the world's largest firms as well as at many conferences. He's going to show you what you need to do in order to make your next speech a success!